Plant Made

Anti-inflammatory Vegan Recipes
Aqsa Liaqat, MD

Let's get it started!

Welcome to Hudson Press. We know how it feels to be the sole decision maker when it comes to food preparation and food budgeting. Given the fact that you are on a diet, or someone in the family is forbidden to eat meat, you are in the process of finding the easiest, simple and delicious vegan recipes to please your picky eaters. It is not easy to think that not all your family members can eat vegan and here's one family member who is on a restricted diet. Stop worrying; here we introduce to you the best vegan recipes that are popular as they are irresistibly delicious and healthy. We know that you are thinking differently, but we assure you that they are not tasteless and bland. Take a look at our 45 vegan recipes, and you will really love them, aside from their delicious tastes, they can be finished in thirty minutes or less!

About This Book

We often hear from some people say, that a vegan diet is something that you will never like because they lack appeal to your taste buds. *Hudson Press* would like to change this notion, which most people think of. We want to change the way you look at vegan dishes because they are far better than some foods that are loaded with fats from meat. We made sure that our 45 collections of easy vegan recipes, are not only healthy, but they can be prepared and cook in thirty minutes or less. While moving away from carnivorous diet, you will be ushered to develop new eating habits that will surely bring good to your health through this cookbook, which is painstakingly written to guide you on the proper way to prepare them, and find other substitute ingredients to suit to your new plant-based diet program. Let's get ready to have a fun time!

CONTENTS

INTRODUCTION

Eating plant-based foods are incomparable when it comes to nutritional value, and how it can help bring back your good health, if ever you are suffering from certain lifestyle diseases. Whatever it is, we introduce to you our 45 easy vegetarian recipes that can be prepared with a total of thirty minutes or less. As a prelude to your new eating habits, we want you to know that some recipes are gluten-free, dairy-free, egg-free, allergen-free, and some are oil-free. If you can't avoid using oil, try olive oil, avocado oil, but refrain from using lard or animal-based oils. You can also use water sauté or cooking in water instead of oil. Some recipes call for vegan cheese, vegan butter, vegan sour cream (cashew sour cream), vegan mayo, cashew mayo, vegan barbecue sauce, extra-firm tofu, hummus, liquid smoke, tamari (gluten-free), tempeh, nutritional yeast, and many more.

Enjoy!

VEGANISM

Introduction:

Veganism is derived from the word "Vegan" which points towards the abstinence behavior from animal products. It is thought to be linked to the use of vegetables and fruits in diet but speaking in a broader definition it is associated with the **"no use of animal products"** in daily life. So people who are following this behavior or lifestyle not only refrain from animal products in their food but also avoid animal's derived products in their clothing, makeup or daily use. Some people following veganism also avoid the products which are tested on animals like certain vaccines, medicines or cosmetics.

History:

History of veganism is not too old. The term was first introduced by "The Vegan Society" in 1944. Until 1949 there was no proper definition of veganism presented by the society. In 1949, a follower of veganism and a member of The Vegan Society pointed that they should have some clear definition of veganism to highlight their cause. So the first definition was "the act of preventing animals from exploitation by men". It was later defined as to seek an end to the use of animals by human beings for the purpose of food, work, experiments, clothing, amusement or any activity that can endanger their species.

The Vegan Society:

The society was reputed as a charity. It was first recognized and registered properly in the August of 1964. Till December 1979 the society worked for the cause of charity and after that the assets were transferred to another society and it became a small company itself.

The definition presented by the vegan society initially was changed and updated over the many years and new definition was presented for veganism in 1988. The new definition is as follows:

"A philosophy and way of living which seeks to exclude—as far as is possible and practicable—all forms of exploitation of, and cruelty to, animals for food, clothing or any other purpose; and by extension, promotes the development and use of animal-free alternatives for the benefit of humans, animals and the environment. In dietary terms it denotes the practice of dispensing with all products derived wholly or partly from animals."

Food options in Veganism:

So now the question may arise in the mind of many readers that what do vegans actually eat if they are avoiding all animal based products? The answer to this question is that there is a whole new world present for the vegans to explore and try. They can choose their food from fruits, pulses, vegetables, nuts, spices etc. anything that do not have any animal product or linked to any animal sacrifice. Following the recipes available especially for the vegans they can prepare their meals including curry, cakes, salads, pasta, pizza etc.

Important reminder:

A follower of veganism does not only avoid the animal products for eating but also has warm feelings in his/her heart regarding the animals. In this way the person raises his/her voice against all the cruel behaviors faced by animals now a day. From sitting on a leather sofa to wearing a leather shoes and jacket an animal has sacrificed his life. Veganism does not allow this kind of behavior. From cosmetics to medicines animals are being sacrificed in trials.

Medical aspects:

Most of the medicines available in the market and formulated by pharmaceutical industries are initially tested on animals worldwide. The vegan society does not recommend followers of veganism to avoid the prescribed drugs by their doctors. The society encourages the followers to seek plant based alternatives wherever possible and request their clinicians to prescribe them those medicines which do not contain animal products like lactose or glucose. In the same way, plant based supplements should be encouraged. But the society does not recommend to avoid medicines or to become non-compliant because a sick vegan or a dead vegan is not the one which is desired by the society. To protect your health always act upon the advice and prescription given to you by your doctor. In fact doctors are not your enemies they are your healers.

Entertainment:

In veganism, people avoid and refrain from all kind of activities that involve exploitation to the animals. So all kind of visits to the animals zoo and aquarium are not desirable for them. They also avoid going to any animal show that causes harm to the animals or compromising the rights of animals. Instead they prefer to visit open areas for rescued animals.

Why to adopt veganism?

One should follow veganism pathway for the following benefits:

1. For the sake of animals
2. For improving your health
3. For saving money
4. For the betterment of environment
5. For other people
6. For your own planet
7. For religious aspects

For the sake of animals:

The followers of veganism believe that human beings are also a type of civilized animal. In this way, the animals should have the equal rights to live their life freely. Almost 60 billion land based animals and more than a trillion marine animals are killed each year to satisfy human taste. This is avoidable because plant derived food and drink are available in all over the world. Animals die before their natural age due to the food acquiring purpose or hunting by the humans.

For improving your health:

Properly planned vegetarian diet recipes are full of nutrients and healthy for your own health. These recipes are appropriate for all the age groups and could easily and effectively replace our animal based diet. Most of the researchers and doctors believe that following a vegan diet plan can provide you with the following benefits:

- Lowering the incidence of hyperlipidemias
- Lowering the blood glucose level
- Prevention from many cancers
- A healthy skin and prevention of many dermatological issues
- A more active and healthy lifestyle

- Increase in the life span
- A better heart and brain
- Better functioning kidneys
- Maintaining a balanced weight
- Prevention of certain food allergies
- Satisfaction of the satiety center
- A controlled blood pressure
- Improvement in vision
- Recovery from joint pains
- Prevention of gynecological problems
- Improving men's sexual health

Lowering the incidence of hyperlipidemias

Certain researches and meta-analysis have found that plant based diets especially the vegan diet is associated with lowering of lipids in the blood. The vegan diets affect both the triglycerides and the total cholesterol in the body. People who are consuming vegan diets are healthy as compared to those who are on omnivorous diet. Vegetables and plant based nutrition are low in lipid content themselves as compared to the meat. That is why they provide you with low levels of fats and lipids. In fact the lipid or cholesterol which is obtained by the plant source either in the form of nuts, oils and fruits is healthy for the human health compared to the lipids which are obtained by animal source. This difference is mainly due to the hydrogen bonding difference present between plant and animal fats. In observational studies it was concluded that plant based diets are responsible for decreasing the total cholesterol to almost 22.9mg/dl as compared to omnivorous diet.

Lowering the blood glucose content

Vegetarian diet or plant based diet is a good source to keep your blood glucose in optimum range. Plant based food has low glycemic index which prevent diabetes mellitus and in patients of already diagnosed diabetes mellitus can keep the glucose level within range. People who adopted veganism can actually maintain their HbA1c level within the desired range. Also patients who are taking insulin in injectable form can lower their required insulin dose by following a vegan diet plan. Plant derived cooking oils like coconut oil and olive oil are also beneficial for the diabetics as compared to the saturated fat and butter.

Most of the nutritionists recommend vegetarian diet or veganism to the patients with uncontrolled diabetes mellitus. Even doctor prefer to treat gestational diabetes mellitus which is a type of diabetes during pregnancy through properly following vegetarian diet plans.

Prevention from Cancers

Cancer is still a leading cause of death worldwide despite the development of certain targeted medicines and therapies. It is a great concern for all the health authorities as well as for the patients and their families. Researchers are working hard to find ways in order to prevent this deadly ailment and to cure it or at least slow down its progress. According to the research data available, the diet is responsible for cancer ailment in 30 to 35% of the cases. Most of the evidences come from the places where purely vegans are living and those societies have less prevalence of different cancers.

Cancer link to meat diet is mostly caused by the processing of meats and their cooking procedures or storage procedures along with their contents. Overall all kind of meat and especially the red meat is associated with increased chances of malignancies. Chicken and other meat containing hormones are a big source of cancer spread in the industrialized world.

A healthy skin and prevention of many dermatological issues

Your skin is the clear depiction of your overall health. A clear and healthy skin reflects that overall a person is enjoying an internally calm health. Any internal disease or problem and even stress is evident from your skin. A vegetarian diet is responsible for giving a healthy glow to your skin and enhancing the overall charm of your personality. Lower level of lipids which is present in plant based diets is very nourishing for the skin. Your skin become dull, oily and often suffers from acne when you rely on animal based food. Contrary to that veganism prevent many skin ailments from acne to malignancies. So adopting veganism can give you a youthful and healthy skin as a reward.

A more active and healthy lifestyle

Overall health of a person is dependent on many things. If you are following a plant based diet or veganism you will feel yourself healthy and active day by day. This kind of lifestyle prevents many diseases and keeps your weight in optimum range which will affect your activity level. A healthy body also has a healthy brain which is free from anxiety and depression. So by following veganism you can enjoy mental health along with physical health. A healthy heart along with healthy joints makes you fit for all the daily activities. You can also reverse and prevent the age related signs in your body by simply following veganism.

Increase in life span

When a person is following simple diet in daily routine with all the nutrients coming from plant sources, he can have a disease free life. By limiting your diseases and preventing them in future through following veganism you can prolong your life span. A disease free person with simple diet has better chances of prolong survival than a person who is taking meat containing food all the day.

A better heart and brain

Heart is the power house of your body. It controls all the blood supply in your body. In case if its supply is compromised for any reason, your whole body will feel a shutdown type situation. Heart is pumping blood after getting it through the blood vessels. It is also dependent on three blood vessels to supply blood for its internal energy. Lipids or fats deposition inside your blood vessels can actually slow down or totally compromise your blood supply to the heart. As a result your heart feels as if it is dying. Initially it can recover from this condition for some time but continuous trauma can lead to permanent disaster. If you are on plant based diets the chances of getting your arteries clogged with lipids are very low. So overall your heart feels better when you are feeding yourself plant based diets. Contrary to that excessive meat consumption can make your arteries flooded with lipids and clog them. This will lead to the disaster for your whole body.

Brain is also dependent on energy supply through blood to properly function. Any compromise in your blood supply to brain can cause the death of the brain tissues which can result in serious problems. Even this can lead to the paralysis of your body. On the other hand veganism can prevent such kind of blood flow compromises in your heart and brain. So you can enjoy better health after following veganism.

Better functioning kidneys

Kidneys can be regarded as the waste disposal system of your body. They help your body to get rid of all the unwanted products in order to maintain balance and harmony inside your body. Any extra burden on your kidneys can make it difficult for them to work efficiently and properly. One of the major function of your body is to get rid of urea and maintaining creatinine in desired range in your blood. Any increase in the levels of urea and creatinine in the blood can result in severe kidney damage.

Meat is the main source of raising urea and creatinine in your body. Initially in young age your kidneys can work extra to get rid of this urea and maintaining the creatinine levels but later on your kidneys can shut down. So nephrologists actually advice their patients to cut down their meat content in meals to avoid this extra burden for the sake of your kidney's health. Renal patients are not allowed to take meat in their meals to keep their urea and creatinine within range.

Maintaining a balanced weight

Human body weight is dependent on the overall calories intake and the type of food you are consuming. The meals which are low in calories and have simple constituents in them can keep a person's body weight within desired range. Consuming the high calorie diet in the form of meaty dishes can disturb your weight. Also consuming high fat dairy products like butter, cheese, cream etc. can contribute to the high calorie intake. They will lead you to the obesity pathway slowly. After getting overweight you will become prone to a large number of diseases and it would become difficult for you to move.

Prevention of certain food allergies

Casein is a milk protein which is considered as a very active allergen from infants to aged people. Beef a type of red meat is also considered as a source of notorious allergens which can lead to severe allergic reactions. Some people also develop allergies to the additional hormones present in the milk and meat of many animals which can endanger their lives.

Many food intolerances are also linked to the consumption of animal products like eggs, honey, lactose etc. On the other hand, veganism is totally a safe approach for most of the people.

Satisfaction of the satiety center

Satiety center is present in your brain. It is responsible for accessing your hunger and sending signals to your body when you feel filled. Any defect in its function can lead to either weight gain or weight loss. When you are on a vegan diet plan your brain feels early that your stomach is properly filled. This will lead to the activation of the satiety center. In this way in fewer calories you can feel a sense of fullness. On the other hand most of the omnivorous diets are high in calories and they do not make you feel satisfied early. This phenomenon will lead you to the obesity pathway.

A controlled blood pressure

Blood pressure is the measure of the pressure faced by your blood to flow in your blood vessels. Any factor that increases the blood pressure will make it difficult for the blood to reach the desired organs and as a result oxygen deficiency and death of the cells occur in the organs. When lipid content is higher in your meals it sticks to the vessel's walls and causes blockage for the blood to flow inside the vessels. So a meaty and high caloric lipid rich meal can elevate your blood pressure and becomes a threat for your life.

Improvement in vision

High lipids diet can lead to increase in the blood pressure which affects the vision badly. Most of the people in old age are suffering from hypertensive eye changes now a day and mostly undergo many surgeries due to this problem. On the other hand plant rich food especially rich in carrots can be very beneficial for the eyes and gives properly required nutrition to the eyes. Carrots are also a good source of vitamin A whose deficiency can lead to night blindness and certain skin diseases.

Recovery from joint pains

Joint pains are mostly caused by the presence of high uric acid in your body. Excessive uric acid can deposit in your joints and makes it very unpleasant for you to move. Uric acid is mostly attained by meat containing meals by your body as an end product of metabolism. So if you avoid the usage of meat in your diet and promote the healthy intake of vegetables, fruits and pulse you can prevent many painful conditions.

Prevention of gynecological problems

Women are facing many gynecological issues now a day which stems out from the improper utilization of food sources. Women health is totally dependent on the proper maintenance of the hormones in the body. Many meat products and milk available now a day are full of bioactive substances and hormones which disturb the internal chemistry of the females. As a result females face many health issues as well as infertility to a large extant. To provide these problems like polycystic kidney disease, infertility, abnormal uterine bleeding etc. you should avoid meat and other animal sources from your diet and replace them from plant based food. As a result you will enjoy a flourished and healthy reproductive life.

Men's sexual health

Most of the meat available now a day is affected by the hormones like prolactin, estrogen to increase the milk production in the animals. These hormones are very harmful for the men's health and their regular consumption can lead to infertility in them. So a better option is to depend on vegan diet to prevent these problems.

Veganism as a source of money saving

We all are well aware of the fact that animal based food and accessories are highly priced. It is not even possible for all to purchase them. Veganism is a source of relief for those individuals who want to save their money and cut down their expenses. In most of the countries fruits and vegetables are 3 to 4 times cheap in prices as compared to meat and poultry. Even plant based oils are cheaper compared to the prices of butter etc.

For saving your planet

Animals are the natural living creatures present on earth. They have got full rights to live their life and enjoy it. Any kind of torture to them or slaughtering these animals for the purpose of getting food or hunting are not justifiable. This kind of injustice can bring anxiety to our planet. So to create a pleasant environment animal's rights must be given. Even hunting of the animals can diminish their valuable species from the planet.

For other people

Adopting veganism can help you and also help those who follow you. If you adopt this lifestyle your family may also follow your foot steps and you can play very positive role in their lives. Following a healthy lifestyle yourself can encourage the people living around you to adopt healthy lifestyle too. In this way you will be a source of spreading health, positive energy and youthfulness as well as saving animals.

Getting complete nutrition from plant based food items

Now we will discuss one by one all the important dietary elements which are required by the human body and how they can be obtained solely from plant based food items. The main nutrients are the following:

1. Carbohydrates
2. Proteins

3. Fats
4. Vitamins
5. Minerals

Carbohydrates

Human body needs carbohydrates to properly function. Most of the activities inside our body are dependent on the proper supply of carbohydrates to the body. Our body needs almost 60 to 70% carbohydrates in a balanced diet. So, most of the meals are composed of carbohydrates. The daily requirement of carbohydrates is around 250 to 350 grams per day. The main sources of carbohydrates from plant derived food items are the following:

- Starchy vegetables like potatoes and corns
- Whole wheat grains, breads and cereals
- Rice
- Legumes of all kinds
- Whole fruits and dry fruits

Proteins

Proteins form the structural and functional components of the human body. Our muscles are the bulk of proteins. Our body obtains energy from protein by running many energy cycles. Proteins are also the part of many hormones, enzymes etc. So proteins are very necessary for the body from hair till your energy cycles. The daily requirement of proteins by your body is described below:

0.75 g/kg per day for women

0.84 g/kg per day for men

1 g/kg per day for pregnant and lactating mothers and also for men and women over 70 years of age

The main sources of proteins from plant based food items are the following:

- Seeds and nuts
- Beans and legumes
- Almond and coconut milk

Fats

Fats and lipids are the second most important component of human diet. They provide cushioning affect to many organs of the body. They also form cell membrane and cell walls of all living cells. They are needed as a source of energy for the body. It is important to maintain a healthy supply of fat in your diet to run all these functions smoothly. They are also important for proper nerve conduction as fats form the nerve sheaths. Around 10 to 15% of your daily diet is composed of fats. Plant derived important sources of fats and lipids are the following:

- Avocado
- Nuts
- Beans
- Coconut oil
- Olive oil
- Mustard oil
- Chia seeds
- Dark chocolate

Vitamins

Vitamins are of two types:

- Water soluble vitamins like vitamin C and vitamin B complex
- Fat soluble vitamins like A, D, E, K

Water soluble vitamins are continuously required by the body to maintain their levels in optimum range. The excess of water soluble vitamins is excreted through kidneys in the form of urine daily. So deficiency of water soluble vitamins can produce side effects rapidly.

Fat soluble vitamins are stored in the fat component of the body. They are stored in the body in excess to what is required by the body. So their deficiency is masked for some time. The excess of fat soluble vitamins can produce serious side effects.

Vitamins are important for the body from maintaining hormones, bones and joints to properly functioning immune system. So deficiency of vitamins produces vast variety of symptoms depending on the type of deficiency. The most important sources of vitamins are the following:

- Fruits
- Vegetables

- Legumes
- Seeds
- Nuts and their oils

Minerals and trace elements

Minerals and trace elements are required in a very low quantity by the body. However their deficiency can lead to severe problems. They range from sodium, potassium, magnesium to copper and zinc.

These minerals are important for the proper functioning of all the muscles, glands and organs in the body. Their deficiency can lead to sudden death especially in children. The main sources of minerals and trace elements are the following:

- Fruits like banana, mango, kiwi etc.
- Vegetables like spinach, green leafy vegetables etc.
- Nuts like cashew nuts, almonds, peanuts etc.
- Legumes and beans
- Oils like almond oil, coconut oil, mustard oil, olive oil etc.

Bottom Line

To summarize the whole discussion in few lines we can say that veganism is a pathway adopted by those individuals who feel pain for animals as well as for their environment. People following veganism refrain and avoid all products derived from animal sources including food and accessories. Veganism is a blessing for improving human health and prolonging disease free lifespan. It can be adopted by anybody to gain the numerous benefits promised by this pathway.

Mexican
Easy Refried Bean Burritos

Originally, this recipe uses cheese, since you are watching your diet, omit the cheese and chicken. Even if there is an absence of meat and cheese, the taste is still flavorful and creamy. This is a perfect vegan burrito that you will ever prepare for your family.

Servings: 12

Ingredients

1 (15-ounce) can **refried beans**

2 cups **cooked brown rice**

1 cup of **salsa**

1 (5-ounce) can diced **green chilies**

1 cup **frozen thawed corn kernels**

12 10-inch **flour tortillas**

½ to 1 teaspoon **ground cumin**

1/4 teaspoon **kosher salt**

1/8 teaspoon freshly **ground black pepper**

Optional toppings:

Salsa

Diced **tomatoes**

Cashew sour cream

Guacamole

Fresh **cilantro**

Diced **avocados**

Sliced **scallions**

Directions

Preheat the oven at 400 degrees Fahrenheit.

Stir in a large bowl the refried beans, salsa, brown rice, chilies, and corn.

Add in ¼ teaspoon kosher salt, 1/8 teaspoon pepper and ½ teaspoon cumin, stir to combine well.

Microwave the tortillas on high for half a second and lay on a flat surface.

Fill each tortilla with 1/3 cup veggie filling right below the center, folding the sides and bring up the bottom part, and then pull tight.

Roll the burrito from its bottom up and tuck the sides.

Place the burritos in a 9by13" pan and bake for twenty minutes until warmed thoroughly and golden brown.

Enjoy!

Nutritional Information: 218 calorie; 2.1 g fat (0.5 g saturated fat); 3 mg cholesterol; 299 mg sodium; 44.4 g carbohydrate; 5.2 g dietary fiber; 1.4 g total sugars; 6.4 g protein.

CAULIFLOWER TACOS

Pretend you are eating tacos with meat filling by preparing these vegan tacos using cauliflower rice, walnuts, chipotle peppers and mushrooms as meat, and the result will drop your jaw. The cooked vegetables are served in tortillas with the optional toppings.

Servings: 6

Ingredients

1 cup **raw walnuts**

3 cups **riced** or **whole cauliflower**

2 tablespoons **water** or **vegetable broth**

4 to 5 medium **white** or **cremini mushrooms**

3 minced **cloves garlic**

1/2 chopped large **red onion**

1 teaspoon **salt**

3 tablespoons **adobo sauce** from the can or jar

2 tablespoons minced **chipotle peppers in adobo**

1 teaspoon **salt**

1 teaspoon **smoked paprika**

2 teaspoons **ground cumin**

6 **flour** or **crunchy corn soft corn tortillas**

Optional ingredients for serving:

Shredded **lettuce**

Chopped **tomatoes**

Non-dairy cheese shreds

Salsa

Avocado slices

Non-dairy sour cream

Directions

Wash whole cauliflower, chop off and put the florets in a food processor.

Pulse the cauliflower to create riced cauliflower, reserving three cups.

Add the mushrooms and walnuts to the food processor. Pulse several times until the mixture has the same consistency of the riced cauliflower, making sure not to over process so as not to turn them into paste.

Heat up a large cast iron skillet on moderate heat.

Pour the vegetable broth or water.

Add the garlic and onion and sauté for two to three minutes until transparent.

Add the cauliflower rice, mushrooms, walnuts, cumin, smoked paprika, chipotles with adobo sauce, and salt to the skillet, stirring often until combined. Cook on moderate heat and stir for fifteen to twenty minutes.

Remove the vegetables from heat.

Serve with corn or flour tortillas and garnish with the toppings of your choice.

Enjoy!

Nutritional Information: 315 calorie; 14 g fat (0.9 g saturated fat); 2 mg cholesterol; 892 mg sodium; 40.6 g carbohydrate; 14.8 g dietary fiber; 13.4 g total sugars; 16 g protein.

Instant Pot Vegan Burritos

Begin your day by filling your body with vegetarian meal, like this vegan burritos cooked in an Instant Pot or you can prepare it without the IP. Whatever it is, the vegan burritos are loaded with tons of vegetables seasoned with medium style salsa, smoked paprika and chili powder.

Servings: 8

Ingredients

For the burrito filling:

2 to 3 tablespoons **water for sautéing** or **olive oil**

1 **red bell pepper**, diced small

1 chopped medium **red onion**

1 (15 ounces) can **drained and rinsed black beans**

3 minced **cloves garlic**

1 1/2 cups **frozen, fresh or canned corn**

1 1/2 cups **uncooked short grain brown rice**

12 ounces **medium style salsa**

1 cup finely chopped **kale**

1 teaspoon **ground cumin**

1 teaspoon **salt**

2 cups **water**

1 teaspoon **smoked paprika**

2 teaspoons **chili powder**

For serving:

8 pieces 10-12" **burrito sized flour tortillas**

1 to 2 sliced or chopped **avocados**

2 to 3 cups chopped **lettuce**

Optional:

Chopped **tomatoes**

Salsa

Chopped **red** or **green onion**

Jalapenos

Vegan cheese shreds

Vegan sour cream

Directions
Instant pot burrito filling:

Prepare the burrito filling by adding olive oil or water to the Instant Pot and press Sauté button.

Add the onion, garlic and red pepper and cook for two to three minutes, stirring often so as not to burn, and turn off Sauté.

Add in the remaining filling ingredients for burrito to Instant Pot, stir and seal.

Set the pot to high pressure for twenty-four minutes, and allow the pressure to release naturally for about ten minutes or so.

Slowly remove the pot's lid, stir the mixture, and add salt or spice according to your taste.

Preparing without Instant Pot:

If you are not using an Instant Pot, cook the filling ingredients in a large saucepan and sauté the onion, garlic and red pepper for a few minutes before adding the remaining ingredients; let boil. Simmer on low for forty-five minutes.

Assemble:

To assemble vegan burritos, fill the center of the tortillas with equal spoonfuls of the filling and place on top the shredded lettuce, avocado slices and toppings.

Fold the two sides of tortilla over the burrito filling and roll up. Serve!

Nutritional Information: 405 calorie; 15.9 g fat (3.2 g saturated fat); 0 mg cholesterol; 1109 mg sodium; 59.7 g carbohydrate; 7.5 g dietary fiber; 4 g total sugars; 10.3 g protein.

Oven Baked Taquitos Recipe

Vegan taquitos could be a healthy option if you are a vegetarian who loves Mexican dishes. Use corn tortillas and fill them with black bean filling and place them in the oven until golden brown. You can either make your own cashew sour cream (see recipe below) or buy a non-dairy version.

Servings: 24 taquitos

Ingredients

4 ounces canned dice & drained **green chiles**

2 (15 ounces) canned drained and rinsed **black beans**

1 teaspoon **chili powder**

3 chopped **green onions**

1/4 teaspoon **garlic powder**

1/2 teaspoon **ground cumin**

1 teaspoon **Sriracha hot sauce**

¼ to 1/2 teaspoon **salt**

½ cup **homemade cashew sour cream** or **store-bought non-dairy sour cream**

24 pieces 6-inch **corn tortillas**

Cashew Sour Cream:

1 1/2 cups **raw cashews**

2 tablespoons of **apple cider vinegar**

3/4 cup **water**

1/4 teaspoon **salt**

1 tablespoon **lemon juice**

Directions

Preheat the oven at 425 degrees Fahrenheit. Cover the bottom of a baking pan with a parchment paper.

Make the filling:

Combine in a large bowl the black beans, green chiles, spices, green onions, sriracha, ½ cup cashew sour cream and salt; stir to combine well.

Cashew Sour Cream:

Do a quick soak for raw cashews by bringing a few cups of water to a full boil and add the 1 ½ cups of raw cashews or you may also place the cashews in a tea kettle filled with boiling water.

Let the cashews soaked with boiling water for five to ten minutes, drain and place in a high powered blender.

Add the apple cider vinegar, salt and lemon juice. Pulse until the mixture is smooth. Keep refrigerated until ready to serve for at least 1 week.

Assemble:

Wrap five tortillas in a moist paper towel at a time, and place in the microwave for thirty seconds to soften.

When the tortillas are soft, fill them with two tablespoons of black bean filling.

Repeat with the rest of corn tortillas and black bean filling. Tightly wrap each tortilla with seam side facing down, on the baking pan.

Bake taquitos for fifteen to twenty minutes until crisp-golden brown. Remove taquitos from oven. Serve with salsa or cashew sour cream.

Serve!

Nutritional Information: 114 calorie; 1.7 g fat (0.8 g saturated fat); 0 mg cholesterol; 62 mg sodium; 20.6 g carbohydrate; 3.8 g dietary fiber; 1 g total sugars; 4.7 g protein.

CHEESY VEGAN QUESADILLAS WITH BLACK BEANS AND VEGETABLES

This thirty-minute vegan dish melts in your mouth with its homemade Mexican cheese made with the combination of nutritional yeasts, raw cashew, salsa and seasonings and pulsed in a food processor. It is used as a coating to the tortillas and topped with vegetables before frying in hot vegan oil or butter.

Servings: 4

Ingredients

Mexican cheese:

1/4 cup **nutritional yeast**

1 1/2 cups **raw cashews**

1/2 teaspoon **ground cumin**

1/4 teaspoon **garlic powder**

6 tablespoons **mild salsa**

1/2 teaspoon **salt**

1/2 teaspoon **chili powder**

Assemble:

3 **mushrooms**, small chops

1 small **zucchini**, small chops

1 (15 ounces) can drained and rinsed **black beans**

2 small **tomatoes**, small chops

1 small **yellow summer squash**, small chops

8 **whole grain or gluten-free tortillas** (8-10 inch size)

DIRECTIONS:
Mexican Cheese:

Place the cashews in a food processor and pulse for three to four minutes until starting to form a buttery texture.

Slowly add the nutritional yeasts, salt, salsa and spices to the food processor and pulse until the mixture forms a creamy and smooth texture, set aside.

For the tortillas:

Place a large pan on a stove and heat up on moderate heat. Coat the pan with oil or vegan butter, shaking the pan to spread out to the sides.

Prepare the tortillas by spreading about 1/3 cup of the Mexican cheese on each tortilla.

Sprinkle on top with the desired amount of black beans, zucchini, tomatoes, summer squash, and mushrooms.

Gently transfer the quesadilla to the pan and cook in batches for two to three minutes until nicely golden, flipping once to cook the other side.

Remove cooked tortilla and cut into wedges. Repeat the same procedure for the rest of the tortillas, Mexican cheese and vegetables.

Serve immediately with vegan sour cream or salsa.

Enjoy!

Nutritional Information: 415 calorie; 25.3 g fat (4.8 g saturated fat); 0 mg cholesterol; 474 mg sodium; 36.2 g carbohydrate; 9.2 g dietary fiber; 6 g total sugars; 17.7 g protein.

Sheet Pan Cauliflower Fajitas

Vegans would surely love this recipe to the max with its aromatic vegetables, roasted in oven and served on tortillas. The hot and spicy salsa is served alongside with guacamole, sour cream and raw vegetables as toppings. There is nothing to worry as the recipe is zero cholesterol.

Servings: 6

Ingredients

1 medium **onion**

1 large head **cauliflower**

2 **green peppers**

2 **red peppers**

2 tablespoon **olive oil** *

1 teaspoon **salt**

Spice mix:

1 teaspoon **cumin**

1 tablespoon **chili powder**

1/4 teaspoon **garlic powder**

1/2 teaspoon **paprika**

1/4 teaspoon **onion powder**

*For oil-free fajitas, use water, instead of oil.

Directions

Prepare the vegetables by chopping into small the cauliflower. Cut the red and green peppers into ¼ inch slices. Slice the onion into lengthwise and cut into ¼-inch slices.

Preheat the oven at 425 degrees.

Spray two small baking sheets or large sheet pan with oil. If you are avoiding oil, cover the sheet pan with a parchment paper or a silicone mat.

Combine the spices in a small bowl, stir to incorporate, set aside.

Put altogether in a large bowl the peppers, chopped cauliflower, spice mixture, onions, salt and olive oil, stir to combine well.

Pour the mixture to the sheet pan and place in the oven to roast for twenty to twenty-five minutes.

Serve vegetables in tortillas together with the beans and rice. Garnish with cashew sour cream, guacamole or your desired toppings.

Serve!

Nutritional Information: 114 calorie; 5.3 g fat (0.7 g saturated fat); 0 mg cholesterol; 446 mg sodium; 16.2 g carbohydrate; 5.5 g dietary fiber; 8.3 g total sugars; 4 g protein.

Quick & Easy Quinoa Tostadas (Gluten-Free, Vegan)

These easy and quick to prepare tostadas are perfect for people who have allergies. They are gluten-free, allergen-free, and vegan. There is no reason to fret when a large crowd will flock to your home to savor this Mexican delight as it can be finished in a total of fifteen minutes.

Servings: 6-8

Ingredients

Filling:

2 bags of **100% quinoa**

1 (15 ounces) can **no-salt added, fire-roasted diced tomatoes**

½ cup chopped **red bell pepper**

½ cup chopped **green bell pepper**

1 teaspoon minced **garlic**

½ teaspoon **chipotle pepper powder**

½ cup chopped **Vidalia onion**

½ teaspoon **smoked paprika**

1 teaspoon **chili powder**

Toppings:

Juice of 1 Lime

Cilantro

1 cup **unsweetened plain coconut yogurt**

6 to 8 **gluten-free corn tostada shells**

Directions

Prepare the quinoa by following the package directions. When done, drain and return quinoa to the large pot, where you cooked it.

Pour the rest of the ingredients for filling, stirring often to incorporate.

Stir in a small bowl the lime juice and coconut yogurt until well blended.

When serving, fill each corn tostada shell with equal amount of quinoa mixture.

Garnish with chopped cilantro and lime yogurt.

Serve!

Nutritional Information: 344 calorie; 11 g fat (4.6 g saturated fat); 0 mg cholesterol; 421 mg sodium; 54.2 g carbohydrate; 5.8 g dietary fiber; 5.1 g total sugars; 7.3 g protein.

CHICKPEA TACOS

A serving of these vegan tacos would be enough to please your hungry guests. Each taco shell or tortilla is packed with cooked chickpeas seasoned with ancho chili powder, cumin, and paprika and lime juice and topped with lettuce, tomatoes and guacamole for extra flavor.

Servings: 2

Ingredients

1 teaspoon **extra virgin olive oil**

2 minced **cloves garlic**

1/2 chopped medium **yellow onion**

Juice of 1/2 lime

1 1/2 cups (1 15 ounce can) drained and rinsed **chickpeas**

1 teaspoon **ancho chili powder**

1/4 cup **water**

1 teaspoon **cumin**

1/2 teaspoon **paprika**

Pinch **salt**

6 **taco shells** or **tortillas**

1/2 cup chopped **tomatoes**

1 cup roughly chopped **green leaf lettuce**

1 batch of **guacamole**

Optional toppings:

Hot sauce

Jalapeño peppers

Cilantro

Directions

Preheat the oven at 365 degrees F.

Heat the extra virgin oil in a large frying pan to moderate heat.

Mince a tablespoon of the onions and set aside. Add the remaining chopped onion to the pan together with the garlic and sauté for five minutes until transparent.

Stir in chickpeas, ancho chili powder, lime juice, paprika, water, pinch of salt and cumin; sauté for ten minutes until thoroughly warmed.

Reduce the heat to low if the chickpeas appear dry and add a spoonful of water. Stir and deglaze the frying pan.

Using fork tines roughly smashed the chickpeas to prevent them from rolling out of the tacos.

Adjust the taste and remove from heat. Heat the tortillas or taco shells in the oven for three to five minutes and remove from oven.

Evenly fill the tortillas or taco shells with the vegetable mixture. Serve with chopped green leaf lettuce, chopped tomatoes, minced onion, and 1 batch of guacamole.

Garnish with optional toppings.

Serve!

Nutritional Information: 1177 calorie; 33 g fat (5 g saturated fat); 0 mg cholesterol; 481 mg sodium; 179.8 g carbohydrate; 43.5 g dietary fiber; 27.1 g total sugars; 47.6 g protein.

ULTIMATE FULLY LOADED VEGAN NACHOS

These nachos call for 1 recipe of Easy Vegan Nacho Cheese sauce, which is provided below and 1 recipe for Cauliflower Walnut Taco Meat with recipe already provided in one of the recipes. Having done the two recipes, arrange the tortilla chips and load with filling and optional toppings.

Servings: 6

Ingredients

1 (16 ounces) bag **tortilla chips**

1 recipe **Easy Vegan Nacho Cheese Sauce**, see recipe below

1 recipe **Cauliflower Walnut Taco Meat** (recipe provided earlier)

2 **roma tomatoes**, diced small

1 (15 ounces) canned drained and rinsed **black beans**

Fresh or jarred and sliced **Jalapenos**

Chopped **green onions**

Cashew sour cream, recipe provided earlier

Diced **avocado** or **guacamole**

Salsa or **hot sauce**

Chopped **cilantro**

Easy Vegan Nacho Cheese Sauce:

3 tablespoons **lemon juice** of 1 large **lemon**

2 cups **raw cashews**

1/2 cup **nutritional yeast**

4 cups **water**, divided

1 teaspoon **garlic powder**

2 teaspoons **salt**

1/2 teaspoon **smoked paprika**

1/2 teaspoon **chili powder**

1 teaspoon **onion powder**

1 to 2 teaspoons **Sriracha** (optional)

Directions
Easy Vegan Nacho Cheese Sauce:

Soak the raw cashews in water overnight or do a quick soak by boiling a pot of water on the stovetop and place the cashews with cover for ten to fifteen minutes and drain.

Transfer the cashews to a food processor and add 3 cups of water, lemon juice, smoked paprika, garlic powder, nutritional yeast, onion powder, salt and chili powder.

Pour the cheese sauce into a medium-sized saucepan. Using a warmed wire whisk, whisk the cheese sauce until bubbly and thickened.

Pour the remaining 1 cup of water to thin out the sauce if it is too thick.

Season the cheese mixture with salt and Sriracha, if you want it a bit spicy. You may refrigerate some leftovers and reheat on the stove with a few drops of water to thin out.

When the nacho cheese sauce is already warm, it is about time to prepare the drained and rinsed black beans and the optional ingredients.

Neatly arrange all tortilla chips on individual or large plate.

Garnish with Cauliflower Taco "meat" (with recipes given earlier in the other page), nacho cheese sauce, black beans, chopped tomatoes, cilantro, minced jalapeños, sliced onions, hot sauce or salsa and cashew sour cream or avocado slices or guacamole.

Serve!

Nutritional Information: 606 calorie; 28.4 g fat (6.4 g saturated fat); 6 mg cholesterol; 1168 mg sodium; 73.5 g carbohydrate; 16.2 g dietary fiber; 5.8 g total sugars; 23.4 g protein.

BBQ Tempeh Tacos and Cabbage

These easy tacos can be prepared in less than 20 minutes. All you have to do is to crumble the tempeh and combine with BBQ sauce in a pan and serve immediately with tortillas and garnished with shredded cabbage.

Servings: 4

Ingredients

1 jar of **BBQ sauce**

1 **block of tempeh**

4 small **tortillas**

1 bag of **shredded cabbage**

Directions

Prepare the tempeh by crumbling into a skillet.

Stir in the BBQ sauce.

Cook on low heat for five to ten minutes, stir and remove from heat.

Place tempeh mixture on tortillas and top with shredded cabbage. Serve warm.

Enjoy!

Nutritional Information: 225 calorie; 9.7 g fat (2 g saturated fat); 0 mg cholesterol; 51 mg sodium; 21.4 g carbohydrate; 2.4 g dietary fiber; 1.9 g total sugars; 17.2 g protein.

ASIAN
RED THAI CURRY VEGETABLES

This authentic Thai curry vegetables are creamylicious and oozing with spices. The mixed vegetables are cooked with coconut milk, Thai red curry paste, tamari, pure maple syrup and lime juice. This is why it is a mixture of something hot, spicy, tangy, and creamy.

Servings: 6

Ingredients

4 minced **cloves garlic**

1 chopped **small sweet onion**

1 **red bell pepper**

1 tablespoon **grated fresh ginger**

1 cup **cauliflower (florets)**

2 medium **carrots**

1 **yellow bell pepper**

1 (15 ounces) can **full fat coconut milk**

1 cup **broccoli (florets)**

2 1/2 tablespoons **Thai red curry paste**

2 cups thinly sliced **kale or spinach**

1/2 cup **water**

2 teaspoons **pure maple syrup**

2 medium diced **roma tomatoes**

1 tablespoon fresh **lime juice of 1 lime fruit**

1 tablespoon **tamari** or **soy sauce**

4 cups cooked **brown** or **white rice**

Optional:

Fresh chopped **basil** or **cilantro**

Sriracha hot sauce

Directions

Cut red and yellow bell peppers into two-inch slices. Peel carrots and cut into small coins or matchsticks.

Prepare the rice by cooking according to its package directions.

Heat up a large pan to moderate high heat and add a few tablespoons of olive oil or water if you want it less oily.

Add the onion and stir for three minutes until transparent. Add the ginger and garlic, stirring for thirty seconds.

Stir in the carrots, bell peppers, cauliflower florets and broccoli. Cook and stir for five minutes, adding a few tablespoons of water if desired. Stir in the curry paste, cook and stir for two minutes.

Add in the coconut milk, kale and water, and bring to a simmer.

Reduce the heat to low and cook with cover for five to ten minutes until all vegetables are tender crisp.

Stir in the tomatoes, fresh lime juice, tamari or soy sauce, and pure maple syrup. Stir to blend the flavors and remove from heat.

Serve with cooked rice and sriracha. Garnish with fresh cilantro or basil.

Enjoy!

Nutritional Information: 705 calorie; 22.3 g fat (16.3 g saturated fat); 0 mg cholesterol; 554 mg sodium; 114.8 g carbohydrate; 8.7 g dietary fiber; 8.2 g total sugars; 13.7 g protein.

Easy Kung Pao Tofu

Experience the taste of Chinese cuisine right in the comfort of your home by preparing this recipe. This recipe is far better than restaurant-bought, with its own homemade recipe for Easy Kung Pao Sauce and top with optional garnishing.

Servings: 4

Ingredients

1 (16 ounces) **block extra-firm tofu**

2 tablespoons **olive oil**

1 large sliced **green bell pepper**

1 large **red bell pepper**

1/3 cup **peanuts**

4 minced **cloves garlic**

1/4 cup **water**

Easy Kung Pao Sauce:

2 tablespoons **rice wine** or **sherry cooking wine**

3 tablespoons **soy sauce**

2 tablespoons **granulated sugar**

1 tablespoon **rice vinegar**

1 teaspoon **Sriracha hot sauce**

1 teaspoon **sesame oil**

1 tablespoon **cornstarch**

1/2 teaspoon **ground ginger**

For optional garnishing:

Sesame seeds

1/4 cup chopped **green onions**

Additional **peanuts**

4 cups cooked **brown** or **white rice**

Directions

Wrap the tofu in a clean cloth or in paper towels slightly pressing and put a heavy object on top. Let tofu sit for one hour to dry.

Combine in a medium-sized bowl the sauce ingredients, whisking to incorporate well.

Now it is time to slice the tofu into three-fourth-inch cubes.

Heat the olive oil in a large skillet on medium high heat.

Place the tofu in the skillet in a single layer and cook for five minutes each side.

Gently flip the tofu using a spatula and cook the other side for another five minutes until both sides are golden-crisp. Remove tofu from skillet and transfer to a plate.

Stir-fry the garlic and bell peppers in the same skillet for two to three minutes.

Pour the homemade Kung Pao sauce to the skillet, stirring often until consistent.

Reduce heat to low and add the peanuts and tofu. Stir and turn off the heat.

Garnish tofu with green onions, additional peanuts and sesame seeds. Serve with steamed rice.

Enjoy!

Nutritional Information: 228 calorie; 15.1 g fat (2.2 g saturated fat); 0 mg cholesterol; 797 mg sodium; 20.7 g carbohydrate; 2.2 g dietary fiber; 11.8 g total sugars; 6.4 g protein.

COCONUT RED CURRY SOUP WITH TOFU IN THE INSTANT POT

The secret to a nicely browned tofu is to wipe it dry and press with a heavy object to remove excess liquid before cooking. In this recipe, the tofu is fried in an Instant pot and cooked with coconut milk, curry powder, baby carrot coins, ginger and turmeric and the broccoli is added just before serving.

Servings: 3

Ingredients

1 block extra firm **tofu**

1 teaspoon **toasted sesame oil**

1 15 ounce can **coconut milk**

1 1/2 cups **water**

2 teaspoons **red curry powder**

1 1/2 cups **baby carrot coins** 1/2"-3/4" thick

1 teaspoon **ground ginger**

1/2 teaspoon **turmeric**

2 cups medium-sized **broccoli florets**

1 **Not-Chick'n Bouillon seasoning cubes** (vegan & gluten-free)

Directions

Press tofu by wrapping in paper towels and put something heavy on top to remove excess water. Dice dried tofu into one-inch cubes.

Heat up the Instant Pot and turn on Sauté mode.

Heat the sesame oil and cook the tofu until golden, stirring often, for five to seven minutes.

Place the remaining ingredients, excluding the broccoli.

Set instant pot at high pressure for four minutes and then with natural release for ten minutes, releasing manually after cooking. Slowly remove the lid and add the broccoli florets.

Cook at high pressure and then make a quick release. Stir to mix the flavors and serve hot!

Enjoy!

Nutritional Information: 570 calorie; 40.1 g fat (31.2 g saturated fat); 0 mg cholesterol; 563 mg sodium; 46.4 g carbohydrate; 14 g dietary fiber; 25.5 g total sugars; 15 g protein.

Easy Vegan Pad Thai (in 30 minutes!)

Your weeknight dinner will never be the same again if you opt to prepare this famous Thai dish. Yup, you can have it in a rush and everyone would be grateful for savoring a spicy and tangy noodles. It calls for Pad Thai Rice Noodles with a piece of Kombu; veggies with sauce and vegan egg scramble.

Servings: 3

Ingredients

For the Noodles:

1 **Kombu**, (optional)

8 ounces **Pad Thai Rice Noodles**

For the vegan egg scramble:

½ teaspoon **salt** or **Kala Namak (Black Salt)**

½ teaspoon **turmeric**

15 ounces **block drained extra firm tofu**

For the vegetables and sauce:

3 tablespoons **coconut sugar**

⅔ cups **vegetable broth**

1 to 3 tablespoons **Sriracha**

2 tablespoons **tamari**

4 minced **cloves garlic**

1 tablespoon **cornstarch plus 3 tablespoons water** or **vegetable broth**

4 **green onions** (separate white and green parts)

1 sliced **red pepper**

Juice of ½ lime fruit

1 cup **bean sprouts**

1 grated **carrot**

Fresh chopped **cilantro** for garnish

Lime wedges for serving

⅓ Cup chopped **dry roasted peanuts**

Directions

Crumble in a small bowl the tofu and add the turmeric, stir to mix well; set aside.

Fill a medium pot with enough water and let boil. Add the Kombu and noodles, cook according to its package directions. Drain the noodles, set aside.

Meanwhile, heat up a large saucepan and splash with water or oil.

Place the crumbled tofu in the saucepan; cook for three to five minutes on medium heat. Sprinkle with ordinary salt or black salt and remove the tofu from saucepan. Set aside.

Splash the saucepan again with water or oil and add the garlic white parts of green onion and garlic; sauté for three minutes until fragrant.

Add the grated carrot and sliced red pepper; sauté for three to five minutes until tender.

To make the Pad Thai sauce, add the coconut sugar, Sriracha, tamari and the vegetable in the same saucepan, stir to combine and bring to a simmer on low heat.

Stir in a small bowl the cornstarch with three tablespoons of water or broth until smooth and pour into the saucepan. Stir and simmer until thickened.

Add the bean sprouts, cooked noodles, green parts of green onions and crumbled tofu. Stir often until well combined and thoroughly heated.

Add the lime juice and remove from heat.

Fill three plates with the Pad Thai and garnish with lime wedges, cilantro and chopped peanuts.

Serve!

Nutritional Information: 612 calorie; 14.7 g fat (2.5 g saturated fat); 0 mg cholesterol; 1021 mg sodium; 102.5 g carbohydrate; 5.7 g dietary fiber; 16.2 g total sugars; 24.7 g protein.

Rainbow Shirataki Bowl with Peanut Lime Sauce

Grab this instagram-worthy Buddha bowl. If you eat this regularly, it will help loosen your weight. Each bowl is filled with colorful vegetables around its sides with Tofu Shirataki Spaghetti in the center. The tangy peanut lime dressing is served right next to your bowl.

Servings: 1 to 2 small bowls

Ingredients

Peanut lime dressing:

2 tablespoons **lime juice from 1 lime**

2 tablespoons **smooth natural peanut butter**

1 teaspoon **Sriracha** (optional)

1/2 teaspoon minced **fresh ginger**

1 tablespoon **soy sauce**

1/2 teaspoon **sesame oil**

1 minced **clove garlic**

For the rainbow bowl:

1 cup shredded **red cabbage**

1 to 2 packages **Tofu Shirataki Spaghetti Shape**

1 peeled and julienned **carrot**

1/2 sliced **red pepper**

1 cubed **mango**

1/3 cup thawed shelled **frozen edamame**

2 chopped **green onions**

1/4 cup chopped **cilantro**

Directions

Combine all ingredients for the peanut lime dressing in a small bowl until incorporated, set aside.

Prepare the rainbow bowl by filling a medium saucepan with water and bring to a boil.

Add the Shirataki noodles and boil for 2 to five minutes until cooked al dente until they are easily separated with a fork. Drain the noodles. Set aside.

To assemble the rainbow bowl, place the cooked noodles in the middle of a large bowl.

Neatly arrange the vegetables according to their kind and color by placing them around the sides of your bowl.

Serve with the peanut lime dressing.

Enjoy!

Nutritional Information: 555 calories; 22.5 g fat (4 g saturated); 82.8 g carbohydrate; 0 mg cholesterol; 1091 mg sodium; 14.8 g dietary fiber; 59.8 g total sugars; 53.3 g protein

Pasta

Instant Pot Vegan Alfredo Sauce

This rich and thick creamy sauce is just the perfect match for your cooked fettuccine pasta. Cook the vegetable sauce in an Instant Pot and blend before pouring over the pasta. Everything will be wiped out and will leave your tongue licking the sauce until no more is left.

Servings: 6

Ingredients

2 tablespoons **olive oil**

6 cups **fresh** or **frozen cauliflower florets**

8 minced **cloves garlic**

½ to 1 teaspoon **salt**

3 cups **vegetable broth**

3/4 cup **raw cashews**

1 pound (16 ounces) cooked **fettuccine pasta**

Optional:

Steamed kale, broccoli or green peas

Directions

Prepare the Instant Pot and press Sauté button.

Heat the olive oil and add the minced garlic.

Cook for 1 to 2 minutes until fragrant, stirring often to prevent burning. Turn off Sauté.

Stir in vegetable broth, raw cashews, and cauliflower florets. Seal and cook on high manual pressure for three minutes. Apply pressure release when it beeps.

Transfer vegetable mixture to a blender, sprinkle with salt and blend until it becomes a smooth paste. Pour into the cooked fettuccine pasta and stir to coat well.

You may add a few tablespoons of water if the sauce is too sticky. Serve pasta with steamed vegetable toppings.

If you are not using Instant Pot, use a large pot and sauté the garlic in hot olive oil, and then add the cauliflower florets, raw cashews, and broth.

Let boil and cook for ten to fifteen minutes and transfer to a food processor and blend until it forms a smooth paste.

Return to the pot and season with salt.

Serve!

Nutritional Information: 534 calorie; 18.5 g fat (2.9 g saturated fat); 0 mg cholesterol; 823 mg sodium; 76.6 g carbohydrate; 4.9 g dietary fiber; 2.8 g total sugars; 15 g protein.

One Pot Pasta with Zucchini, Garlic Scapes, and Leeks in a White Wine Lemon Sauce

A candlelight dinner would be more intimate by having this one pot pasta with vegetables cooked in white wine, lemon juice, almond milk and a host of spices and seasonings. The creamy white sauce is the secret why this pasta dish is unbelievably the best.

Servings: 4

Ingredients

2 teaspoons **olive oil**

12 ounces **whole wheat rigatoni**

2 **leeks** white and light green parts

1 large **zucchini** cut into quarter moons

1 small bunch **garlic scapes**

1 teaspoon **dried oregano**

1/4 teaspoon **red pepper flakes**

Pinch **ground black pepper**

1/4 teaspoon **salt scant**

1 tablespoon **lemon juice**

2 cups **low-sodium vegetable broth**

1 teaspoon **lemon zest loosely packed**

1/2 cup **plain unsweetened almond milk**

1/2 cup **white wine**

Fresh basil

Directions

Heat olive oil in a large saucepan over medium heat.

Cook the chopped leeks with minced garlic, in case garlic scapes are unavailable; stirring often and cook for three to five minutes until softened.

Add the rigatoni, zucchini, garlic scapes, lemon zest and spices.

Pour vegetable broth, white wine, lemon juice, and almond milk over the rigatoni mixture; bring to a boil and simmer on low heat.

Partially cover the saucepan and stir often for 7 to 10 minutes until the pasta is cooked al dente and the sauce has thickened.

Adjust the taste by adding salt. Serve pasta with fresh basil.

Serve!

Nutritional Information: 376 calorie; 6 g fat; 243 mg sodium; 67 g carbohydrate; 5 g dietary fiber; 2 g total sugars; 11 g protein.

THAI CURRY FETTUCCINE

Delight your loved ones with this extra delicious fettuccine, cooked with Thai curry, which is a blend of curry paste, curry powder, coconut milk, peas, and seasoned with sugar and tamari. This authentic Asian flavor is a blend of sweet, spicy, creamy with a crunchy texture.

Servings: 6

Ingredients

1 tablespoon **extra-virgin olive oil**

16 ounces **fettuccini**

4 finely chopped **cloves garlic**

1/2 cup (diced small) **red bell pepper**

1/2 teaspoon **sea salt**

1 teaspoon **curry powder**

1/4 cup **red curry paste**

28 ounces (2 cans 14 ounces each) ounces **coconut milk full fat**

(17% to 22%) coconut milk (cream)

3 tablespoons **brown sugar packed**

1/4 cup **soy sauce** or **tamari**

1/2 cup **peas frozen**

1 (8 ounces) can sliced and drained **bamboo shoots**

Directions

Prepare the fettuccine by cooking according to its package directions.

Heat the oil in a large pan and cook the red bell pepper for ten minutes. Stir in garlic and cook for 1 minute longer.

Add in curry powder, salt, coconut milk, soy sauce, red curry paste, and brown sugar.

Cook and stir on medium low heat for ten minutes. Stir in peas and bamboo shoots; cook for five minutes.

Add the cooked fettuccine and toss to coat well.

Serve!

Nutritional Information: 476 calorie; 15 g fat (10 g saturated fat); 63 mg cholesterol; 671 mg sodium; 68 g carbohydrate; 3 g dietary fiber; 9 g total sugars; 12 g protein.

PESTO PASTA WITH ROASTED BRUSSELS SPROUTS AND TEMPEH SAUSAGE

This pasta recipe is a complete meal with flavorful roasted Brussels sprouts, tempeh sausage and pesto poured over the pasta. It is zero-cholesterol and can be done quickly in 55 minutes, and it can feed a throng of diners.

Servings: 8-10

Ingredients

Pesto:

1½ cups **raw cashews**

3 cups **loosely packed fresh basil**

2 **cloves garlic**

⅓ cup **fresh lemon juice**

4 tablespoons **nutritional yeast**

½ to 3/4 teaspoon **salt**

¼ to ½ cup **water**

Roasted Brussels sprouts:

1 pound **fresh** or **frozen Brussels sprouts**

Spray of olive oil (optional)

Tempeh Sausage:

1 tablespoon **fennel seed**

8 ounces cubed **tempeh**

1 teaspoon **oregano**

1 teaspoon **basil**

2 minced **cloves garlic**

½ teaspoon **red pepper flakes**

½ squeezed **lemon**

2 tablespoons **soy sauce**

1 pound **whole wheat** or **gluten-free pasta**

Directions

Preheat the oven at 425 degrees Fahrenheit.

Pesto:

Soak the raw cashews in hot water for about twenty minutes to 1 hour.

Place cashews and the remaining pesto ingredients in a food processor. Pulse until smooth, set aside.

Roasted Brussels sprouts:

Trim and cut into half the Brussels sprouts.

Line a sheet pan with silicone mat or spray with olive oil and place the sprouts, with cut side down.

Lightly spray the sprouts with olive oil and roast for twenty minutes. You have the option to omit spraying with olive oil if you want it oil-free.

Tempeh sausage:

Place the cubed tempeh in a small pan with enough water to cover.

Simmer on medium heat for ten minutes until the liquid is almost absorbed.

Add the rest of the sausage ingredients, cook on medium heat and stir for five minutes until lightly browned.

Pasta:

Cook the pasta al dente, drain and return to the pot where you boiled it. Pour the pesto sauce, tempeh sausage mixture and roasted Brussels sprout over the cooked pasta.

Serve!

Nutritional Information: 964 calorie; 52 g fat (9.8 g saturated fat); 0 mg cholesterol; 788 mg sodium; 99 g carbohydrate; 16.9 g dietary fiber; 18.4 g total sugars; 36.3 g protein

LEMON ONE POT PASTA

What a better way to enjoy pasta without the meat is by preparing this zesty one pot pasta, which is packed with nutrients and flavors. You don't look for other dishes since this is a complete meal that can sustain your energy all day long.

Servings: 4

Ingredients

8 ounces **spaghetti**

2 chopped **leeks** (use the lower and lighter part)

2 1/4 cups **vegetable broth**

Juice of 1 to 1 ½ lemons

1 cup drained and rinsed **chickpeas**

1/2 tablespoon **garlic powder**

2 1/2 tablespoons **nutritional yeast**

1 teaspoon **Dijon mustard**

1/2 tablespoon **onion powder**

1 large handful **spinach**

1/2 cup **frozen peas**

Toppings:

Vegan Parmesan

Directions

Combine in a large saucepan all ingredients excluding the spinach and peas; bring to a boil.

Cook on medium heat for another ten minutes until the pasta is almost cooked al dente, stirring often.

When almost done, add the spinach and peas until thoroughly heated.

Remove from heat and garnish with vegan Parmesan.

Serve!

Nutritional Information: 216 calorie; 2.2 g fat (39.5 g carbohydrate); 6.75 g dietary fiber; 11 g protein.

Whole Wheat Penne with Mushrooms, Spinach, and Tomatoes

This hearty pasta dish is cooked in avocado oil and seasoned with Italian seasoning blend and dry white wine. Instead of meat, it is substituted with baby mushrooms and cooked with baby spinach, tomatoes, and spices until the sauce has thickened and poured over the cooked whole wheat penne.

Servings: 4

Ingredients

2 tablespoons **avocado oil**

13 ¼ ounces **whole wheat penne pasta**

1 thinly sliced **shallot**

5 minced **cloves garlic**

1 pound rinsed and lightly patted dry **baby 'bella mushrooms**

1/3 cup **dry white wine**

3/4 teaspoon **kosher salt**

1 tablespoon **Italian seasoning blend**

5 ounces **baby spinach**

1 (28 ounces) can diced **tomatoes with juice**

1/4 teaspoon **freshly ground pepper**

Directions

Fill a large pot with salted water and cook the pasta according to the package instructions, drain and set aside.

Heat the avocado oil in a large pan and cook the shallot and garlic for 2 to 3 minutes until fragrant and soft.

Add in the wine, let simmer for two minutes.

Add in the mushrooms, salt, Italian seasonings and pepper, stirring often, until the flavors are fully blended. Cook and stir often for 6 to 8 minutes until the mushrooms have shrunk and tender.

Stir in the tomatoes with juices; simmer on low for ten minutes until the sauce has slightly decreased.

Stir in the spinach until starting to wilt for two to three minutes.

Toss the penne pasta to the mixture until coated well.

Serve!

Nutritional Information: 478 calorie; 12 g total sugars; 15.9 g fat; 71 g total carbohydrates; 21 g protein.

Butternut Squash Mac and Cheese

Enjoy more servings of this delicious vegetable dish guilt-free as it does not use any dairy product to enhance its creaminess. It is the powerful combination of cashews, boiled butternut squash, nutritional yeasts, Dijon mustard, seasonings and lemon juice that makes the mixture thick and consistent plus the peas and noodles.

Servings: 6

Ingredients

1/2 cup **raw cashews**

1 medium chopped **butternut squash**

2 tablespoons **cornstarch**

2 cups **water**

1 tablespoon **Dijon mustard**

1/2 cup **nutritional yeast**

1 teaspoon **onion powder**

1/2 teaspoon **garlic powder**

1 1/2 teaspoon **salt**

2 tablespoons **lemon juice**

16 ounces **whole grain** or **gluten free elbow noodles**

2 cups **frozen peas**

Directions

Prepare the butternut squash by removing the skin and cut into medium-sized chunks.

Place the squash in an Instant Pot and add two cups water. Cook for eight minutes on high pressure. If you don't have an Instant Pot, you can roast, boil or steam the squash until tender.

Prepare the pasta by filling a large pot with water and bring to a full boil. Cook the elbow noodles for seven minutes.

Add the two cups frozen peas, cook for two minutes longer.

Drain the peas and noodles together in a colander and return to the pot.

Meanwhile, place the cooked squash in a blender together with the remaining ingredients, excluding the peas and noodles. Process until the mixture is smooth.

Pour into the pot with the peas and noodles. Stir to combine all ingredients on low, medium heat for one to two minutes until the mixture is consistent.

Serve!

Nutritional Information: 751 calorie; 9 g fat (1.2 g saturated fat); 0 mg cholesterol; 665 mg sodium; 135.4 g carbohydrate; 23.7 g dietary fiber; 7.1 g total sugars; 35.3 g protein.

Vegan Spaghetti

Your little ones will love this vegan spaghetti with its yummy taste and saucy texture, even if it is meatless and without the cheese. The marinara sauce, consisting of vegan meatballs, spices and tomatoes are pour over the cooked pasta.

Servings: 4

Ingredients

1 tablespoon **olive oil**

400 grams **spaghetti noodles**

1 pack **marinara sauce**

Optional **vegan meatballs**

1 chopped **red onion**

2 crushed **clove garlic**

1 diced **tomatoes**

Mushrooms

Shredded **spinach**

Directions

Cook the spaghetti noodles according to its package instructions, drain and return to pot.

Heat the olive oil in a large pan and sauté the crushed garlic, chopped onion, tomatoes, mushrooms, vegan meatballs, and spinach, stir often to incorporate.

Pour the marinara sauce to the mixture. Cook and stir often, and add salt and pepper.

Pour the mixture over the cooked pasta.

Serve!

Nutritional Information: 555 calorie; 15.9 g fat (1.1 g saturated); 74 mg cholesterol; 706 mg sodium; 75.6 g carbohydrate; 6.7 g dietary fiber; 8.4 g total sugars; 29.3 g protein.

Burgers
Best Veggie Burger Recipe (Vegan & Grillable)

These versatile vegetable burgers can be cooked in oven, stove top or grill, and it is up to you to choose the toppings and sauce for variation, such as mayo sauce, guacamole or barbecue sauce. They are a healthy alternative while you satisfy your burger cravings.

Servings: 12 burgers

Ingredients

1/4 cup **ground flax**

3 (2 15-oz cans, drained and rinsed) cups cooked **black bean**

1/2 cup **water**

1 1/2 cups cooked **brown rice**

1 cup **cashews**

1 1/2 cups shredded **carrots**

1/2 cup chopped **parsley**

1/3 cup chopped **green onions**

2 tablespoons **smoked paprika**

1 cup **bread crumbs**

1 to 2 teaspoons **salt**

1 tablespoon **chili powder**

Directions

Stir in a small bowl the ground flax with ½ cup of water, set aside.

Place in a large bowl the black beans and mash with a fork or potato masher until almost all the beans become a paste, leaving one-fourth whole.

Put the cashews in a food processor, pulse until they turn into bread crumb size, and some are whole to add coarse texture to your filling.

Add the cashews to the beans, stir to combine and add the flax mixture and the remaining ingredients.

Combine the ingredients with a large spoon and shape into 12 equal size burger patties with 3/4 –inch thickness.

Cooking on stove:

Heat 2 to 3 tablespoons of oil on the stove on medium heat and add four burger patties in one sitting. Cook for four minutes each side until golden-crisp. Flip and cook the opposite side and transfer to a plate covered with a paper towel.

Cooking in oven:

Preheat the oven at 350 degrees F. Cover the bottom of a baking sheet with a parchment paper and place the burger patties. Bake for twenty minutes, flipping once and bake for fifteen minutes more. Remove patties from oven.

Cooking on the grill:

Chill the patties for half an hour to firm up. Heat up the grill over medium high heat and brush the burger patties with oil. Grill the patties for four minutes per side.

To assemble:

Place patties on bun bottoms and followed by vegan mayo, ketchup, mustard, slices of pickles, lettuce leaf, tomato slices and onion; cover with top bun.

Enjoy!

Nutritional Information: 375 calorie; 8.1 fat (1.6 saturated fat); 0 mg cholesterol; 477 mg sodium; 61.9 g carbohydrate; 10.7 g dietary fiber; 3.1 g total sugars; 16.2 g protein.

The BEST Bean Burgers

This vegan, oil-free, gluten-free bean burger is considered as the best of all bean burgers despite its few ingredients to make the patty. These are the kidney beans, mustard, quick oats, ketchup, onion powder, and garlic powder.

Servings: 4 burgers

Ingredients

1 (15 ounces) can drained and rinsed **kidney beans**

1 teaspoon **garlic powder**

1 tablespoon **mustard**

1/3 cup **gluten-free quick oats**

2 tablespoons **ketchup**

1 teaspoon **onion powder**

Directions

Preheat the oven at 400 F.

Coat a large baking sheet with oil or line with a parchment paper, set aside.

Place the beans in a large mixing bowl and mash until everything becomes a smooth paste. Add the remaining ingredients, stirring to combine well.

Divide the mixture into four and roll them into balls. Place the balls on the baking sheet and flatten out with your palms.

Bake the patties for ten minutes and gently flip after ten minutes to cook the other side for another ten minutes.

Serve!

Nutritional Information: 133 calorie; 0 g fat (0 g saturated fat); 153 mg sodium; 25 g total carbohydrates; 7 g dietary fiber; 3 g total sugars; 7 g protein.

INSTANT POT PULLED BBQ JACKFRUIT

Jackfruits are not only healthy, but they can be used to create a faux pulled meat by cooking in an Instant Pot and mashed afterwards and then cooked again with your homemade vegan barbecue sauce. Place the pulled BBQ jackfruit on buns with shredded cabbage.

Servings: 6

Ingredients

2 (20 ounces) cans **young green jackfruit in brine** or **water**

18 ounces **barbecue sauce** (See accompanying recipe below)

6 **gluten-free hamburgers**

Shredded **cabbage**

Quick and easy vegan barbecue sauce:

2 tablespoons **molasses**

2 cups **organic ketchup**

1/4 cup **apple cider vinegar**

2 teaspoons **Sriracha**

1/4 cup **brown sugar** or **pure maple syrup**

2 tablespoons **vegan Worcestershire sauce**

2 tablespoons **low sodium soy sauce**

Directions
Prepare the jackfruit:

Drain and rinse the jackfruit, removing the core and discard. Place the jackfruit in the Instant Pot with 1 cup of water.

Cover the lid, and turn on high pressure for five minutes. Let the pressure release naturally or do it manually. Slightly cool and drain the jackfruit and return to the pot.

Using a potato masher, mash the jackfruit until it looks like pulled meat. Set aside.

Pour the barbecue sauce into the Instant Pot and press Sauté feature. Cook the mixture for two to five minutes until thoroughly warmed.

Served pulled jackfruit on hamburger buns and garnish with shredded cabbage.

Quick and easy vegan barbecue sauce:

Combine in a medium-sized bowl, all ingredients for the sauce, whisking to combine well. This recipe will yield about 2 ½ cups of sauce. Keep refrigerated for up to one week.

Enjoy!

Nutritional Information: 468 calorie; 5.6 g fat (1.1 g saturated fat); 0 mg cholesterol; 2379 mg sodium; 102.7 g carbohydrate; 13.6 g dietary fiber; 53.9 g total sugars; 6.1 g protein.

KIDNEY BEAN BURGERS

Love these plant-based burgers with all your heart. They are quick to prepare and only call for six ingredients, including the kidney beans. Combine all ingredients and form them into patty and bake. There you have your instant vegan, fat-free, cholesterol free, gluten-free and vegan burger delights.

Servings: 4

Ingredients

1 (15 ounces) can **drained and rinsed kidney beans**

1/3 cup **gluten-free quick oats**

1 tablespoon **yellow mustard**

2 tablespoons **ketchup**

1 teaspoon **onion powder**

1 teaspoon **garlic powder**

Directions

Preheat the oven at 400 degrees F and spray your baking sheet with cooking spray. Set aside.

Place the beans in a large mixing bowl, and mash with potato masher until it becomes a smooth paste. Add the remaining ingredients, stir to coat well.

Apportion the bean mixture into four equal parts. Roll them into balls and place on the baking sheet. Flatten out the balls using your palm.

Bake for ten minutes, and gently flip and bake the other side for ten minutes.

Serve!

Nutritional information: 127 calorie; 0.5 g fat (0.1 g saturated fat); 0 mg cholesterol; 172 mg sodium; 22.7 g carbohydrate; 8.9 g dietary fiber; 3 g total sugars; 7.6 g protein.

Veggie Bean Burgers

These high fiber vegan burgers will perk up your day with its load of vegetables, herbs, spices and seasonings. The beans and vegetables are roasted separately in the oven and pulse together with the tomato paste, panko breadcrumbs and other ingredients. Serve this on bread rolls with the vegetable toppings.

Servings: 8 burgers

Ingredients

1 medium **carrot**

8 ounces **mushrooms**

1/4 medium **onion**

1 1/2 cups **broccoli florets**

2 tablespoons **avocado** or **olive oil**

2 medium **garlic cloves**

1 teaspoon **chili powder**

1 teaspoon **smoked paprika**

1/4 teaspoon **fresh ground black pepper**

3/4 teaspoon **fine sea salt**

1/3 cup **walnut halves**

1 (15 ounces) can **drained and rinsed black beans**

Handful **fresh herbs like chives, parsley or cilantro** (optional)

2 cups **packed spinach leaves**

1 tablespoon **tomato paste**

1/2 cup **panko breadcrumbs**

3/4 cup cooked **brown rice**

8 **bread rolls**

Toppings:

Lettuce

Tomato

Cheese

Burger sauces

Directions

Heat the oven at 400 degrees F. Cover the bottom of two rimmed baking sheets with silicon baking mats or foil.

Rinse the mushrooms, brushing the dirt out and cut away to remove its hard stems.

Chop the onion, broccoli, carrot, mushrooms into one-half-inch chunks and place in a food processor.

Add in the olive oil, garlic, chili powder, smoked paprika, pepper and salt and then pulse for ten to twenty times until coarsely ground, making sure they don't turn into a paste.

Pour the coarsely ground veggies into the baking sheet and spread evenly. Roast the mixture for fifteen minutes, stirring and pressing from time to time to prevent burning and then spread the mixture again.

Evenly spread the drained and rinsed black beans on the second rimmed baking sheet and roast for fifteen minutes, stirring and pressing and then spread into one layer.

Return the two baking sheets to the oven and roast for fifteen minutes until dry and toasted. Remove from oven and let cool.

To make the burgers:

Rinse and pat dry the food processor. Put together the walnuts, fresh herbs and spinach in the processor and pulse until the mixture resembles the size of bread crumbs.

Add in the cooled beans and pulse for five to ten times until the beans form into large crumbs.

Add in the roasted veggies, tomato paste, panko breadcrumbs and pulse, so that all ingredients are incorporated.

Scrape the mixture into a large bowl and combine with the rice. Chill the veggie burger overnight.

Assemble:

Divide the veggie patties into eight equal amounts and form into one-half-inch thick patties.

Heat the avocado or olive oil in a large skillet on medium low heat.

Cook four burgers at a time until both sides are browned for four to six minutes per side.

Serve veggie burgers on bread rolls and top with vegetable toppings.

Serve!

Nutritional Information: 216 calorie; 22 g carbohydrate; 12 g fat (2 g saturated fat); 47 mg cholesterol; 381 mg sodium; 5 g dietary fiber; 2 g total sugars; 8 g protein.

SALADS

QUICK & EASY WHITE BEAN SALAD (VEGAN, GLUTEN FREE)

You have a total of 5 minutes to prepare this salad by combining the salad ingredients and in a separate bowl, combine the dairy-free yogurt dressing and pour over the salad. If you are using pita pockets, tuck in the lettuce leaf in the pocket and load with the salad. The nutritional info does not include the pita pockets.

Servings: 4

Ingredients

For the white bean salad:

1 1/2 cups cooked **white beans** or 1 (15 ounces) can **rinsed and drained beans**

1/4 cup diced **red bell pepper**

1/2 cup diced **cucumber**

2 tablespoons **fresh chopped parsley**

2 chopped **green onions**

For the tangy dairy-free yogurt dressing:

Juice of 1/2 lemon

1/4 cup **dairy- free unsweetened plain yogurt**

1 teaspoon **Dijon mustard**

Pinch of salt & pepper

For the pita sandwich:

4 **pita pockets**

4 leaves of **red leaf lettuce**

Directions

To prepare the white bean salad, mix all its ingredients in a mixing bowl and set aside.

Combine in a small bowl, all ingredients for the yogurt dressing and pour over the white bean salad, tossing to coat well.

To serve on pita pocket, tuck one leaf of lettuce into individual pita pocket and fill with the white bean salad.

Serve!

Nutritional Information: 186 calorie; 2 g fat; 587 mg sodium; 32 g total carbohydrates; 9 g dietary fiber; 2 g total sugars; 9 g protein.

VEGAN CHICKEN SALAD WITH PICKLES

This easy and no cook vegan chicken salad is prepared by combining the salad ingredients and poured with the dressing. Please see notes below on how to prepare the soy curls, or Beyond Meat or garbanzo beans for the salad. You can pick any of them for this recipe.

Servings: 3

Ingredients

For the dressing:

1 tablespoon **mustard**

1 minced **clove garlic**

3/4 cup **vegan mayo** (see recipe in another page)

1/2 teaspoon **salt**

1 tablespoon **pickle juice from jar of dill pickles**

For the salad:

1/2 cup diced **dill pickles**

1(8 ounces) **bag of soy curls or 1-2 bags frozen Beyond Meat strips/ 2 cans drained garbanzo beans***

4 sliced **green onions**

4 diced **stalks celery**

Handful of **parsley**

For serving:

Pretzel buns

Lettuce leaves

Avocado slices

Directions

For the dressing:

Whisk in a small bowl, all the dressing ingredients, set aside.

For the salad:

Place soy curls or any of your prepared protein in a mixing bowl and add in the celery, pickles, parsley and onions. Pour the dressing all over the salad mixture, and toss to coat well. Serve on pretzel bun with lettuce leaves and avocado slices.

*Notes:

Preparing the Soy Curls:

Place in a bowl of water the dehydrated soy curls and soak for fifteen minutes until soft. Drain and squeeze out excess water. Chop and mix with the salad ingredients.

Preparing the Beyond Meat:

Prepare Beyond Meat by following the package directions, and heat them in a skillet over medium heat, chop into bite size and combine with the salad ingredients.

Preparing the garbanzo beans:

Drain two cans of garbanzo beans and mash with a fork and combine with the salad ingredients.

Enjoy!

Nutritional Information: 445 calorie; 16.5 g fat (0.1 g saturated fat); 0 mg cholesterol; 1464 mg sodium; 63.8 g carbohydrate; 4.2 g dietary fiber; 1.3 g total sugars; 14.9 g protein.

ASIAN VERMICELLI NOODLE SALAD

The Italian pasta is given an Asian touch by filling the salad with myriads of veggies, such as carrots, cucumber, bell pepper, cilantro, roasted peanuts and scallions and top with homemade spicy peanut sauce. It is a bit spicy and flavorful that will surely become a megahit in your home.

Servings: 4

Ingredients

Vermicelli Salad:

1 cup shredded **carrots**

8 ounces **vermicelli noodles**

1/2 thinly sliced **cucumber**

1 seeded and thinly sliced **red bell pepper**

1/2 cup **cilantro**, loosely packed

1/4 cup **dry roasted peanuts**

3 chopped **scallions**

Peanut Sauce:

2 tablespoons **soy sauce**

3 tablespoons **natural peanut butter**

2 **cloves garlic**

1 tablespoon **rice vinegar**

1 teaspoon **Sriracha** or similar **hot sauce**

1 tablespoon **fresh ginger**

1/4 cup **water**

Directions

Prepare the vegetables by chopping the cucumber, bell pepper and carrots.

Cook the noodles in salted boiling water for two to three minutes, stirring until there are no more clumps.

Remove noodles from heat, strain and rinse in cold running water; set aside.

Mix in a food processor all peanut sauce ingredients and blend until it forms a smooth peak.

Pour the peanut sauce over the cooked noodles and add the vegetables, roasted peanuts, scallions and cilantro. Toss to combine well and chill until ready to serve.

Enjoy!

Nutritional Information: 371 calorie; 11 g fat (2 g saturated fat); 778 mg sodium; 59 g carbohydrates; 4 g dietary fiber; 5 g total sugars; 9 g protein.

Vegan Egg Salad

Egg salad without the egg, is what this recipe all about. It uses a block of dried and crumbled extra firm tofu to resemble like an egg consistency and mixed with the nutritional yeast, Dijon mustard, vegan mayo, celery, seasonings and turmeric. You will like its taste without noticing the absence of egg.

Servings: 4

Ingredients

1 **block extra firm tofu**

1 tablespoon **low-sodium soy sauce**

1 diced **stalk celery**

1 1/2 tablespoons **Dijon mustard**

1 1/2 tablespoons **nutritional yeast**

1/2 teaspoon **turmeric**

2 tablespoons **relish**

2 tablespoons **vegan mayo**

1/4 teaspoon **onion powder**

1/4 teaspoon **garlic powder**

Directions

Drain the tofu by wrapping in a clean dish towel.

Put a heavy object on top of the tofu block to let the excess liquid to drain out ten to fifteen minutes.

Pat the tofu with paper towels and crumble into a mixing bowl with your clean hands to achieve a real egg salad consistency.

Add in the remaining ingredients, mix thoroughly until incorporated.

Serve!

Nutritional Information: 115 calorie; 5 g fat (1 g saturated fat); 0 mg cholesterol; 340 mg sodium; 7 g total carbohydrates; 2 g dietary fiber; 2 g total sugars; 12 g protein.

Vegan Tomato Cucumber Feta Salad

This summer prepare a vegan salad by making a tofu feta using drained and pressed extra-firm tofu with coconut vinegar, dried oregano and sea salt. Combine the tofu feta with the cucumber & tomato salad seasoned with red wine vinegar and olive oil.

Servings: 4

Ingredients

For the Tofu Feta:

1/4 cup **coconut vinegar**

1 pound **extra-firm tofu**

1/4 teaspoon **sea salt**

1 1/2 teaspoons **dried oregano**

For the salad:

1 sliced **English cucumber** or 2 to 3 **Persian cucumbers**

1 dry pint **cherry** or **grape tomatoes** halved

2 tablespoons **red wine vinegar**

1 tablespoon **olive oil**

Fresh basil leaves

Pinch of **salt and pepper** to taste

Directions

Drain and press the tofu and slice into cubes.

Place tofu in a Ziploc bag and add in the salt, oregano, and coconut vinegar. Seal the bag and shake to combine well.

Chill for two hours or overnight for extra flavor.

Combine in a salad bowl the Tofu Feta, cucumbers, and tomatoes; drizzle with red wine vinegar and olive oil.

Add a pinch of salt and pepper, toss to combine. Garnish salad with fresh basil leaves.

Enjoy!

Nutritional Information: 108 calorie; 5 g fat; 5 g total carbohydrates; 219 mg sodium; 2 g total sugars; 8 g protein.

SUMMER GREEK PASTA SALAD

Stay fresh and hydrated during hot season by preparing this quick and easy pasta salad that can be done in a total of 12 minutes. Combine all vegetables, homemade salad dressing and cooked pasta and serve with a dollop of cream cheese or feta.

Servings: 4-6

Ingredients

400 grams **bow pasta**

12 **cherry tomatoes**

1/2 **cucumber**

6 tablespoons **dairy-free cream cheese**

16 **green pitted olives**

Salad Dressing:

Handful of **flat leaf parsley**

4 tablespoons **olive oil**

Dash of **ground black pepper**

1 tablespoon **red wine vinegar**

Directions

Prepare the bow pasta by cooking in a large saucepan filled with boiling water, al dente. Drain the pasta and rinse under cold running water. Place in the colander to remove the remaining liquid, set aside.

Prepare the vegetables by cutting the cucumber in half lengthwise. Scoop out the cucumber seeds and discard.

Chop the parsley into small squares and cut the cherry tomatoes in half.

Whisk in a small bowl the red wine vinegar, black pepper and olive oil.

Toss the pasta in a large mixing bowl with the vegetables and the dressing.

Serve in individual bowls with dollops of cream cheese or diced feta.

Enjoy!

Nutritional Information: 567 calorie; 22.9 g fat (7 g saturated fat); 81 g carbohydrate; 12.9 g protein; 4.7 g total sugars.

Vegan Crispy Garlic Tofu

There are only three ingredients to come up with crispy and delicious tofu. Each tofu cube is spiced up with garlic powder, nutritional yeast and liquid aminos before baking. Serve it with steamed rice and vegetables of your choice.

Servings: 2

Ingredients

1 tablespoon **nutritional yeast**

1 block **extra firm tofu**

2 tablespoons **liquid aminos**

1 tablespoon **garlic powder**

Directions

Preheat the oven to 450 degrees.

Press the tofu for one hour to remove excess water. Cut tofu into bite-sized cubes.

Place on a baking sheet, and sprinkle with garlic powder and nutritional yeast, tossing gently to coat the tofu cubes.

Pour liquid aminos into the mixture and toss to coat well. Bake for fifteen.

Remove the tofu from oven and shake the pan to flip the cubes or use tongs. Bake for fifteen minutes more.

Remove tofu from oven and serve with rice and vegetables.

Enjoy!

Nutritional Information: 73 calorie; 3 g fat (0.3 g saturated fat); 0 mg cholesterol; 968 mg sodium; 6.9 g carbohydrate; 1.9 g dietary fiber; 1.3 g total sugars; 9.4 g protein.

SANDWICHES
VEGAN BLT SANDWICH WITH BAKED TEMPEH BACON

BLT sandwiches can be enjoyed even if you are on a restricted diet by preparing a vegetarian version. This recipe calls for a Smoky Baked Tempeh Bacon (with recipe below) and Tofu Vegan Mayonnaise (with recipe below), and then assemble all the ingredients in your bread slices.

Servings: 5 sandwiches

Ingredients

1 batch **Tofu mayo** or **store bought vegan mayo**

1 batch **Smoky Baked Tempeh Bacon**, see recipe below

3 to 4 large sliced **ripe tomatoes**

1 to 2 heads **romaine** or **iceberg lettuce**

8 to 12 slices **sourdough bread** or **any bread**

Optional:

Avocado slices

Sprouts

Smoky Baked Tempeh Bacon:

2 (8 ounces) packages **tempeh**

3 teaspoons **liquid smoke**

1/2 cup **apple cider vinegar**

1/2 cup **low sodium soy sauce**

1/2 teaspoon **cumin**

2 tablespoons **pure maple syrup**

Tofu Vegan Mayonnaise Recipe (Oil Free):

1 (12.3 ounces) package **Mori-Nu Silken Firm Tofu**

1/4 teaspoon **salt**

2 tablespoons **fresh lemon juice**

1/2 teaspoon **agave** or **pure maple syrup** (optional)

1 teaspoon **Dijon mustard** or **yellow mustard**

Directions
Smoky Baked Tempeh Bacon:

Prepare the tempeh by slicing into one-fourth-inch very thin slices to come up with 12 strips per package or a total of 24 strips.

The easiest method to do is to cut the bacon tempeh block in half, and then slice into thin strips.

Now, it is time to prepare the marinade by mixing the apple cider vinegar, soy sauce, pure maple syrup, liquid smoke and cumin in a medium-sized bowl, whisking well to incorporate.

Neatly arrange the tempeh strips in a 13x9" baking dish. Pour the marinade over the tempeh strips and marinate for one hour or overnight.

Preheat the oven at 350 degrees Fahrenheit.

Cover the bottom of a large baking sheet with a parchment paper and place the tempeh strips on the pan.

Bake the tempeh strips for fifteen minutes, flip and bake for another fifteen minutes. Remove from oven.

Tofu Vegan Mayonnaise Recipe (Oil Free):

Place all ingredients including the tofu in a food processor; blend until smooth. Pour into a glass container and refrigerate for up to 1 week. This tofu vegan mayo can be used in preparing burgers, sandwiches, coleslaw dressings, fruit salad or potato salad.

To assemble:

After making the tempeh bacon and vegan tofu mayo, it is time to toast the bread and then layer with your homemade vegan mayo or store-bought, tempeh bacon, lettuce, tomato and the optional toppings.

Serve!

Nutritional Information: 398 calorie; 3 g fat (0.9 g saturated fat); 0 mg cholesterol; 833 mg sodium; 70.1 carbohydrate; 9.4 g dietary fiber; 10.3 g total sugars; 22.9 g protein.

VEGGIE SANDWICHES

This is the simplest sandwich recipe that you can do in less than ten minutes. Layer the hummus on the bottom of the bread and then followed by the vegetables in any particular order. You can use this recipe for burgers, wraps and sandwiches.

Servings: 1

Ingredients

1 **sourdough** or **Dave's Killer Bread**

2 tablespoons **hummus**

1 **lettuce leaf**

½ **red onion** slices

1/2 cup **drained and rinsed black beans**

1/2 thinly shredded medium **carrot**

1/4 thinly sliced **bell pepper**

1/4 thinly sliced **cucumber**

1/4 sliced **avocado**

Handful of **mustard green raw**

Directions

Slice sourdough or Dave's Killer Bread into halve.

Spread the hummus on the bottom and layer with lettuce leaf, red onion slices, black beans, carrot, bell pepper, cucumber and sliced avocado.

Add on top a handful of mustard and top with the other half of bread.

Serve!

Nutritional Information: 704 calorie; 15.2 g fat (3.2 g saturated fat); 0 mg cholesterol; 557 mg sodium; 114.2 g carbohydrate; 23.5 g dietary fiber; 8.7 g total sugars; 33.1 g protein.

THE BEST AND EASIEST CHICKPEA TUNA SALAD SANDWICHES

These faux tuna salad sandwiches are made to imitate the flaky texture of a real tuna by combining the mashed chickpeas with your homemade vegan mayo, dill pickles, soy sauce or tamari with celery if you wish. They are best served in sandwiches, burgers, wraps, rolls or salad bowl.

Servings: 6

Ingredients

1 to 2 medium **dill pickles**, small chops

1 tablespoon **tamari (for gluten-free)** or **soy sauce**

2 (15-ounce) cans drained and rinsed **chickpeas (garbanzo beans)**

3 to 4 tablespoons **vegan mayo** (see recipe below)

1/4 cup **celery**, small chops (optional)

For serving:

Bread

Sliced **tomatoes**

Lettuce

Red onion

Avocado

Mustard

Optional Cashew Mayo:

1 **cup raw cashews**

1/2 teaspoon **salt**

2 tablespoons **fresh lemon juice**

1/2 cup **water**

1/2 teaspoon **ground mustard**

2 tablespoons **apple cider vinegar**

Directions

Mash in a large bowl the chickpeas using fork tines or potato masher until almost all beans are mashed, leaving a few whole for added appeal.

Combine the mashed beans with pickles, 3 to 4 tablespoons of homemade vegan mayo, celery and soy sauce (tamari), stirring to coat well.

Cover the mixture and chill for half an hour, or until ready to serve.

Serve with bread slices, mustard, lettuce leaf, tomato slices, onion slices and avocado slices. It is up to you if you wish to serve this in a wrap, or in a large green salad bowl.

Prepare cashew mayo:

Soak raw cashews in hot water for five to thirty minutes and drain.

Place drained cashews and the remaining mayo ingredients in a food processor.

Blend for a few minutes until smooth. Leftover mayo can be stored in the fridge for one week.

Serve!

Nutritional Information: 426 calorie; 20.1 g fat (4 g saturated fat); 0 mg cholesterol; 1036 mg sodium; 51.5 g carbohydrate; 7.2 g dietary fiber; 5.9 g total sugars; 12 g protein.

Wraps
Hummus Vegetable Wrap

Make it a habit to prepare a healthy vegan wrap like this recipe. It is best for your lunch or supper and you can eat as much as you can as it is spread with hummus and stuffed with black beans, carrot, bell pepper, brown rice, cucumber and avocado.

Servings: 1

Ingredients

1 package **brown rice**

1 **whole-wheat or gluten-free tortilla**

2 tablespoons **hummus**

1 cup **spinach**

1/2 cup **drained and rinsed black beans**

1/2 thinly sliced medium **carrot**

1/4 thinly sliced **bell pepper**

1/4 thinly sliced **cucumber**

1/4 sliced **avocado**

Directions

Prepare the rice by cooking according to its package directions.

Place the tortilla in a microwave and warm up for fifteen seconds.

Spread the hummus in the center of tortilla, and then top with spinach, ¼ cup brown rice, drained and rinsed black beans, carrot, bell peppers, cucumber and avocado slices.

Gather the edges of the tortilla and fold.

Flip one side of tortilla over and roll to resemble a burrito; wrap in foil.

Serve!

Nutritional Information: 834 calorie; 16.6 g fat (3 g saturated fat); 0 mg cholesterol; 172 mg sodium; 144.5 g carbohydrate; 25.2 g dietary fiber; 6.9 g total sugars; 32.6 g protein.

KOREAN TEMPEH LETTUCE WRAPS

If you've been obsessed with Korean wave, it is pretty sure; you are familiar with some Korean dishes that making waves in the cooking arena. One of them is this crunchy and tangy lettuce wraps filled with pickled radishes & onions, Sriracha mayo and tempeh. The nutritional info is based on 6 servings.

Servings: 6 to 8 wraps

Ingredients

For the pickled radishes and onions:

½ cup **water**

1½ cups **distilled white vinegar**

1 tablespoon **salt**

2 tablespoons **sugar**

½ sliced large **red onion**

8 thinly sliced **radishes**

For the tempeh:

2 tablespoons **soy sauce**

2 tablespoons **brown sugar**

1 (8 ounces) **crumbled package tempeh**

2 tablespoons minced **garlic**

For the sriracha mayo:

½ teaspoon **sriracha**

½ cup **vegan mayo**

Directions

Prepare a small saucepan and add the vinegar, sugar, water and salt, bring to a boil. Simmer on low heat until both sugar and salt are dissolved.

Pour into a bowl with onions and radishes; toss and cool for fifteen minute. Place in the refrigerator for forty-five minutes.

Mix in a medium-sized bowl, all ingredients for tempeh, tossing to coat well and marinate for half an hour.

Heat a few drops of oil in a large pan and cook the tempeh for five to eight minutes.

Add in the Sriracha and vegan mayo.

To assemble the wrap, lay out the leaves of lettuce on a work surface and top with cooked rice, tempeh, pickled radishes and onions, Sriracha mayo sauce and cilantro.

Enjoy!

Nutritional Information: 394 calorie; 19.9 g fat (4.5 g saturated fat); 0 mg cholesterol; 1647 mg sodium; 25.6 g carbohydrate; 0.5 g dietary fiber; 8.6 g total sugars; 24.9 g protein.

Pizza
Easy Pita Bread Pizza

Vegan pizza means so much if you are following a healthy lifestyle. This recipe uses pita bread as a base for your pizza and spread with Daiya or non-dairy cheese shreds before topping with herbs, spices and vegetable toppings.

Servings: 1

Ingredients

1 **pita bread**

1/4 cup **non-dairy cheese shreds, Daiya** or **Follow Your Heart**

2 tablespoons **spaghetti** or 2 tablespoons **pizza sauce**

Dash of **oregano**

Dash **basil**

Dash **garlic powder**

Olive oil (optional)

Toppings:

Mushrooms

Tomatoes

Spinach

Chopped small **broccoli**

Green pepper

Directions

Preheat the oven at 400 degrees F.

Brush the pita with a little olive oil and spread the pizza sauce on top.

Sprinkle on top of sauce the shredded Daiya and then top with pinches of spices and herbs and add the suggested toppings or your choice.

Place pita pizza on a baking sheet. Bake for five to seven minutes until the cheese has melted.

Remove pizza from oven and slice with a pizza cutter.

Enjoy!

Nutritional Information: 383 calorie; 17.4 g fat (3.1 g saturated fat); 0 mg cholesterol; 523 mg sodium; 51.2 g carbohydrate; 6.7 g dietary fiber; 8.4 g total sugars; 9.4 g protein.

Rice

Easy Beans and Rice

This meatless bean and rice recipe is versatile in the like that it can be served for breakfast, brunch, lunch or supper. This one-dish meal can be prepared in a jiffy by using canned black beans and cooked together with the rice, veggie stock, salsa, and vegetables. Serve it with your favorite sauce.

Servings: 2

Ingredients

1 (15 ounces) canned **drained and rinsed black beans**

1 cup **uncooked quick rice or frozen pre-cooked rice**

 2 ½ cups **vegetable stock**

1 chopped **avocado**

1 serving **salsa**

2 **lettuce leaves**

1 **tomato chunks**

Hot sauce for serving

Directions

Drain and rinse the black beans and heat up in a medium-sized saucepan on medium heat.

Add the rice to the beans, stir to coat well.

Pour the vegetable stock and simmer on low heat, stirring often.

Add the chopped avocados, tomato chunks, shredded lettuce and salsa and, stir to combine well.

Season the vegetables with salt and pepper and add the hot sauce if you wish.

Serve!

Nutritional Information: 783 calorie; 24.7 g fat (6.8 g saturated fat); 0 mg cholesterol; 1394 mg sodium; 124.4 g carbohydrate; 20.5 g dietary fiber; 7.6 g total sugars; 22.7 g protein.

Kimchi "Fried" Rice

This quick and easy rice recipe can be done in fifteen minutes. All you have to do is heat the frozen veggies, scallions, rice, tofu, vegetable broth and season with tamari and add the kimchi just before serving and sprinkle with toasted sesame.

Servings: 4

Ingredients

1 cup **frozen vegetables (organic carrot, pea, and corn mix)**

1/4 to 1/2 cup **vegetable broth**

4 chopped **scallion stalks**

2 tablespoons **tamari** or soy sauce

2 cups cooked **brown rice**

1/4 cup **kimchi**

5 to 7 ounces package of **firm pre-baked tofu cubed**

1 teaspoon **sesame seeds** (optional)

Directions

Put altogether in a large skillet the frozen vegetables and scallions with vegetable broth and heat thoroughly, stirring often to combine well.

Add the brown rice and tamari (soy sauce) and add some more vegetable broth if needed.

Stir in tofu, cook and stir until thoroughly heated. Remove mixture from heat and stir in kimchi.

Sprinkle with toasted sesame seeds.

Enjoy!

Nutritional Information: 233 calorie; 3.5 g fat; 38.5 g total carbohydrate; 5 g dietary fiber; 12.5 g protein.

BEANS

VEGAN STOVE-TOP SMOKY RED BEANS

Dinner is getting exciting when everybody knows you are serving them with these smoky red beans cooked with blended vegetables and seasoned with Cajun seasoning, liquid smoke, marjoram and spices. Serve these spicy beans with Instant Pot Dirty Rice.

Servings: 6

Ingredients

1 cup minced **onion**

2 tablespoons **coconut oil** or **water sauté**

1/2 cup **celery**

1 cup minced **bell pepper**

1 1/2 teaspoons **Cajun seasoning**

1 teaspoon minced **garlic**

1/2 teaspoon **thyme**

1 teaspoon **marjoram**

1 teaspoon **liquid smoke**

1/4 teaspoon **black pepper**

3 (15 ounces) cans drained and rinsed **Harris Teeter Organic Dark Red Kidney Beans**

1/2 cup **Harris Teeter Organic Vegetable Broth**

Pinch of **salt**

1 **bay leaf**

Hot sauce of your choice

Directions

Heat the coconut oil in a medium-sized saucepan and add the onion.

Sauté until translucent and then add the celery, garlic, bell pepper and Cajun seasoning; stir until the vegetables are soft and the spices are aromatic.

Stir in the vegetable broth, liquid smoke, pepper, thyme, marjoram and cook for five minutes longer.

Pour the mixture into a food processor and blend until smooth and pour into the saucepan.

Add the red kidney beans and bay leaf to the saucepan; stir and cook for fifteen minutes on low heat until the beans are heated thoroughly and the flavors are blended.

Serve over Instant Pot Dirty Rice or steamed rice.

Enjoy!

Nutritional Information: 238 calorie; 4.6 fat (3.9 g saturated fat); 0 mg cholesterol; 616 mg sodium; 36.9 g carbohydrate; 10.8 g dietary fiber; 5.4 g total sugars; 12 g protein.

Baked Beans and Baked Potatoes with Steamed Broccoli

These baked potatoes are filled with canned vegetarian baked beans and served with steamed broccoli. They taste so good, even without seasonings and other ingredients, and they are an excellent meal for people with restricted diet.

Servings: 4

Ingredients

1 (16 ounces) can **vegetarian baked beans**

4 **Russet potatoes**

12 ounces fresh or frozen small **head broccoli**

Pinch of **coarse salt**

Dash of **ground pepper**

Directions

Prepare the broccoli by cutting into small florets.

Bake the russet potatoes for 1 hour at 350 degrees Fahrenheit. You can also microwave the potatoes for five to six minutes after poking with a fork, turning once and microwave the other side.

Steam the broccoli florets and sprinkle with salt and pepper. Warm the beans.

Cut open the baked potatoes and fill with warm beans.

Serve potatoes with steamed broccoli.

Enjoy!

Nutritional Information: 267 calorie; 0.8 g fat (0.1 g saturated fat); 0 mg cholesterol; 475 mg sodium; 60.2 g carbohydrate; 10.8 g dietary fiber; 12.1 g total sugars; 10.1 g protein.

Conclusion

Thank you so much for downloading this eBook. We at Hudson Press hope this book has increased your knowledge regarding some tasty, easy vegan recipes that can be prepared in 30 minutes or less. This eBook contains a curated list of what we believe to be the 45 best vegan recipes which encompass a variety of methods, flavors and tastes. All different categories of vegan dishes are represented such as your vegan burger, vegan sandwich, vegan rice, vegan soup, vegan pasta, vegan taco, vegan burrito, and many more.

While doing our extensive research, we made sure that all ingredients are not hard to find, and that the recipes should be simple, easy and quick to do. We made sure that the vegan ingredients are explained well, so as not to confuse you from their non-vegan counterparts. Since we understand your goal to stay healthy, we came up with our best recipes that are not only delicious, but they are great sources of nutrients. This book provides vast information about your searches. We wish you luck in your journey towards a healthy diet, by digesting all information found in our recipes.

Thanks again for your support.

Happy Cooking!

Made in the USA
San Bernardino, CA
24 November 2019